Amir Nizar Zuabi

I Am Yusuf And This Is My Brother

Methuen Drama

Published by Methuen Drama 2010

1 3 5 7 9 10 8 6 4 2

Methuen Drama
A & C Black Publishers Limited
36 Soho Square
London W1D 3QY
www.methuendrama.com

ISBN 978 1 408 13005 6

A CIP catalogue record for this book is available from
the British Library

Typeset by Country Setting, Kingsdown, Kent CT14 8ES
Printed and bound in Great Britain by
CPI Cox and Wyman, Reading RG1 8EX

This book is produced using paper that is made from wood grown
in managed, sustainable forests. It is natural, renewable and recyclable.
The logging and manufacturing processes conform to the environmental
regulations of the country of origin.

I Am Yusuf And This Is My Brother

by Amir Nizar Zuabi

This production opened at the Al Midan Theatre, Haifa, on 24 September 2009, then toured to towns and villages in Galilee and the West Bank. It opened at the Young Vic, London, on 19 January 2010.

I Am Yusuf And This Is My Brother

by **Amir Nizar Zuabi**

Ali **Ali Suliman**

Yusuf **Amer Hlehel**

Rufus **Paul Fox**

Old Nada / Woman from different time / Um Samar / Water woman / Dead refugee **Salwa Nakkara**

Nada / Water woman / Dead refugee **Samaa Wakeem**

Nagi / Water woman / Dead refugee **Taher Najib**

Girl from Haifa / Water woman / Dead refugee **Tarez Sliman**

Old Yusuf / Man with tree / Man from Haifa **Yussef Abu Warda**

Direction **Amir Nizar Zuabi**
Design **Jon Bausor**
Light **Colin Grenfell**
Music **Habib Shehadeh Hanna**
Stage manager **Vicky Berry**
Deputy stage manager **Lauren Rose Shalabi Patman**

We are grateful to many individuals, foundations, companies and public funders for their support of *I Am Yusuf And This Is My Brother*. In particular the Young Vic and ShiberHur wish to thank

Supporters of the Young Vic's international programme

Esmée Fairbairn
FOUNDATION

Supporters of the associated learning programme

clore duffield foundation

Production supporters

THE LINBURY TRUST

In addition, we are grateful to the following people for their generosity: Robert Fox, Helena Kennedy QC, Roger Lloyd Pack and Jehane Markham, and Vanessa Redgrave.

When I started writing this play I had one image in my head: my father waking up as a small child and seeing that his home town of Nazareth had turned overnight into a huge refugee camp; looking out of the window and seeing his city had changed . . . A moment ago he was sleeping, breathing gently encased by innocence, and now war had become part of his life and at once the eyes of that boy were pricked by a thorn of pain – that thorn is still there in my father's gaze and I inherited that thorn that pricks in the eye whenever we look at this land . . . Our land.

We that have stayed are plagued by ghosts: the ghosts of the people that left, and the ghosts of what could have been. We that still walk around the relics of our shattered dream have a responsibility not to turn 1948 into a dream or a legend, even just because of this simple fact: we know that walking up the stairs of the deserted neighbourhoods in Haifa in the humidity of August is hard; you sweat and you wish you were living in Switzerland; but then you look back, and you see the gulf of Haifa and the sea . . . and then the thorn pricks your eye, reminding you to ask yourself –

What if ?
What could have been?
Where are the people who sweated like me?
Where are they now?

This play is about them: people, just ordinary people – complicated and beautiful – who led a life that was their own and who now lead a life of 'what if'.

AMIR NIZAR ZUABI,
Haifa, December 2009

GLOSSARY

The Koran verses in the play are all from Surah Yusuf.

Places mentioned in the play

Baissamoon (and Amuka) – small villages in the Galilee, in the Saffad area. They were destroyed in 1948.

Dair Yassin – a small village near Jerusalem. The people of the village were massacred in 1948 – only a few survived.

Manara – the central square of Ramallah.

Led and al Ramlah – two major cities in the centre of Palestine. They were rich with citrus groves. They fell in 1948. The majority of their inhabitants now live in the West Bank refugee camps.

Acre – historic port town in the north of Palestine, a stronghold for the crusaders. The most beautiful of the ancient cities and the most ancient of the beautiful cities.

Hit-tin – the battle grounds where Saladin defeated the Crusaders on the 4 July 1187.

Arabic words and phrases

Allah yerhamu – May he rest in God's mercy

Tfadlu – Welcome

Mafashets guli – I still didn't empty my anger

Bissmillah – In the name of Allah (God)

Allah hu Akbar – Allah (God) is great

Debbka – A traditional line dance

Ya hallaly – A traditional wedding song

Ashad ana la illaha ela Ilah and muhamed rasul Allah – There is no god but Allah and Mohamed is his prophet. The proclamation that every Muslim has to say.

Qaougji warriors – Local Palestinian soldiers fighting in the 1948 war, led by Fauzi al Qaougji.

Hejira – The departure of the prophet Mohamed from Mecca to Medina in 622, considered to be the birth of Islam.

Jon Bausor Design

Jon trained on the Motley Theatre Design Course in London.
Theatre includes: *The Winter's Tale* (RSC); *Kursk* (Young Vic / Sound&Fury);
Scenes From the Back of Beyond (Royal Court); *The Soldier's Tale* (Old Vic);
The Birthday Party (Lyric Hammersmith).
Dance includes: *The Tale of Two Cities* (Northern Ballet Theatre);
Opera includes: *The Knot Garden* (Klangbogen Festival, Vienna);

Paul Fox Rufus

Theatre includes: *Salonika* (West Yorkshire Playhouse); *SOAP* (Northampton
Theatre).
Television includes: *Moving On*; *Casualty*; *The Royal*; *Coronation Street*;
City Central; *Hearts and Minds*.
Film includes: *Hero*; *Simon*.

Colin Grenfell Light

Theatre includes: *365*; *The Bacchae*; *Black Watch* (National Theatre of
Scotland); *Single Spies* (Theatre Royal Bath); *Riflemind* (Trafalgar Studios);
Kes (Royal Exchange, Manchester); *Playing the Victim* (Told By An Idiot).
Opera includes: *La Bohème* (English Touring Opera); *The Thief of Baghdad*
(Royal Opera House), and extensive work for Opera Holland Park.

Habib Shehadeh Hanna Music

Studied music in the Composing Centre in Jerusalem and is director and
founder of Al Mashgal Music Centre.
Theatre includes: *Jidarriya*; *Diab*; *Blood Wedding*; *That's the Tale*;
War or More.
Film includes: *The Lemon Tree*; *The Band's Visit*.
Albums include: *Baldna, Ya Taier Gane*.

Amer Hlehel Yusuf

Trained at Haifa University.
Theatre includes: *War or More*; *Sneeze and Other Shorts* (ShiberHur);
Forget Herostratous (Al Midan, Haifa).
Film includes: *Paradise Now*; *America*; *Time Remaining*.
As a director: *Shokran*; *Song of Songs*; *The Rose Fields*.

Taher Najib Nagi / Water woman / Dead refugee

Theatre includes: *Peer Gynt*; *Medea Al-Zir Salem*.
Film includes: *The Olive Harvest*; *I, Frank*.
As a director: *I Will Betray My Land*.
As a playwright: *Wall of the Sea*; *Spitting Distance*.

Salwa Nakkara Old Nada / Woman from different time / Um Samar / Water woman / Dead refugee

Trained at Bait Zvi Drama Studio.
Theatre includes: *Them; Out* (Neve Sedek); *Jerusalem Syndrome; August Moon Café* (Haifa Municipal); *Black Rain* (Hertzelia Ensemble); *The House of Bernarda Alba; The Glass Menagerie; Accidental Death of an Anarchist* (Midan Theatre); *Ghosts* (Palestinian National Theatre).
Film includes: *Pink Subaru; A Narrow Bridge.*

Tarez Sliman Girl from Haifa / Water woman / Dead refugee

Studied music at Haifa University.
Theatre includes: *The Devil's Dance; Diab; The Horn Blower; The Rose Fields.*
Albums include: *Ya Taier Gane; Al Musher Al Sagier.*

Ali Suliman Ali

Trained at Yoram Levenstein Studio.
Theatre includes: *The Key of the Heart; The Glass Menagerie; Waiting for Godot; The Tempest; A View from the Bridge; Forget Herostratous; Salome; Sneeze and Other Shorts.*
Television includes: *Bazel; War on Jerusalem; In Real Time.*
Film includes: *Paradise Now; Body of Lies; The Kingdom.*

Samaa Wakeem Nada / Water woman / Dead refugee

Studied drama at Haifa University and dance / ballet at Gatton Academy.
Theatre includes: *Houash;* The *Voyage of Compassion.*
Dance includes: *Al Sira Wal Massira* (Remaz Dance Company); *Love is My Faith* (Sufi Dance); *Sirhan and the Pipe* (Jawal Theatre).

Yussef Abu Warda Old Yusuf / Man with tree / Man from Haifa

Trained at the Bait Zvi Drama Studio.
Theatre includes: *Saved; The Maids; The Crucible* (Beersheba Municipal Theatre); *Waiting for Godot; The Caretaker* (Haifa Municipal); *Black Rain; Antigone* (Hertselia Ensemble).
Television includes: *Ezra Safra & Sons; File Closed.*
Film includes: *Nadia; A Narrow Bridge; The Promised Land.*

Amir Nizar Zuabi Playwright / Direction

Trained as an actor at the Nisan Nativ drama studio and is founder of the ShiberHur Company.
As a director, theatre work includes: *Alive from Palestine; When the World was Green* (Young Vic); *Stories Under Occupation* (Al Kassaba, Ramallah); *Voligo Andare In Prigone* (Collosseo Theatre, Rome); *Jidaria - Mahmoud Darwish* (Palestinian National Theatre); *Forget Herostratous; Tale of Autumn* (Al Midan, Haifa) *War or More; Sneeze and Other Shorts* (ShiberHur); *Samson and Delilah* (Vlamsse Opera House).
As a writer, work includes: *Clinging on Stone; Album; War or More; I Am Yusuf and This Is My Brother.*

ShiberHur

ShiberHur – [Shib-ër-Hûhr] 'an inch of freedom'

A compound of **Shiber** (an Ottoman measuring unit equal to an open palm) and **Hur** (Arabic for 'free').

ShiberHur is a new independent Palestinian theatre company based in Haifa and dedicated to producing the very best of contemporary and classical theatre for audiences across Palestine and abroad.

In 2008 a group of leading theatre practitioners, led by Amir Nizar Zuabi, founded ShiberHur to create a truly independent space where they can create high standard theatre. ShiberHur is an emerging and constantly evolving ensemble of performers and collaborators. Our mission is to break new ground, broaden access to theatre, generate new loyal audiences and foster a love for quality theatre in Palestine.

The Young Vic and ShiberHur wish to thank supporters of the project in Palestine:

F o n d s

Prince Claus Fund *for*
Culture and Development

الصندوق العربي للثقافة والفنون
The Arab Fund for Arts and Culture

Culture Resource

مؤسسة عبد المحسن القطان
A.M. Qattan Foundation

THE YOUNG VIC

GREAT SHOWS FOR GREAT AUDIENCES
NOW AND IN THE FUTURE

Our shows
We present the widest variety of classics, new plays, forgotten works and music theatre. We tour and co-produce extensively within the UK and internationally.

Our artists
Our shows are created by some of the world's great theatre people alongside the most adventurous of the younger generation. This fusion makes the Young Vic one of the most exciting theatres in the world.

Our audience
... is famously the youngest and most diverse in London. We encourage those who don't think theatre is 'for them' to make it part of their lives. We give 10% of our tickets to schools and neighbours irrespective of box office demand, and keep prices low.

Our partners near at hand
Each year we engage with 10,000 local people – individuals and groups of all kinds including schools and colleges – by exploring theatre on and off stage. From time to time we invite our neighbours to appear on our stage alongside professionals.

Our partners further away
By co-producing with leading theatre, opera, and dance companies from around the world we challenge ourselves and create shows neither partner could achieve alone.

Thank God for the Young Vic. *The Observer*

One of Britain's most consistently imaginative theatres. *Daily Telegraph*

The Young Vic is a company limited by guarantee, registered in England No. 1188209.
VAT registration No. 236 673 348
The Young Vic (registered charity number 268876) receives public funding from:

SUPPORTING THE YOUNG VIC

The Young Vic relies on the generous support of many trusts, companies, and individuals to continue our work, on and off stage, year on year.

For their recent support we thank

Public Funders
Arts Council England
Equalities and Human
  Rights Commission
London Development Agency
Southwark Council

Corporate Supporters
American Airlines
Bupa
Bloomberg
Cadbury Schweppes
  Foundation
De La Rue Charitable Trust
HSBC Bank plc
J.P. Morgan
KPMG Foundation
London Communications
  Agency
London Eye
North Square Capital

The Directors' Circle

Big Cheeses
HgCapital
Ingenious Media plc
Land Securities

Hot Shots
Clifford Chance
Slaughter and May
Taylor Wessing LLP

Trust Supporters
The Arimathea Charitable
  Trust
The City Bridge Trust
City Parochial Foundation
John S Cohen Foundation
Columbia Foundation Fund
  of the Capital Community
  Foundation
Dorset Foundation
D'Oyly Carte Charitable Trust
Equitable Charitable Trust
Eranda Foundation
Ernest Cook Trust
Esmée Fairbairn Foundation
Garrick Charitable Trust
Genesis Foundation
Goethe-Institut
Help a London Child
Henry Smith Charity
Jerwood Charitable
  Foundation
John Ellerman Foundation
John Thaw Foundation
The Limbourne Trust
Man Group plc Charitable
  Trust
Martin Bowley
  Charitable Trust
Peter Moores Foundation
Quercus Charitable Trust
Steel Charitable Trust
The Worshipful Company
  of Grocers

Production Partnership
Tony & Gisela Bloom
Sandy Chalmers
Kay Ellen Consolver
  & John Storkerson
Eileen Glynn
Chris & Jane Lucas
Nadine Majaro
  & Roger Pilgrim
Anda & Bill Winters
Miles Morland
Mr & Mrs Roderick Jack

Best Friends
Jane Attias
Chris & Frances Bates
Alex & Angela Bernstein
The Bickertons
Katie Bradford
Sarah Hall
Richard Hardman & Family
Nik Holttum
  & Helen Brannigan
Suzanne & Michael Johnson
Tom Keatinge
John Kinder & Gerry Downey
Carol Lake
Tim & Theresa Lloyd
Simon & Midge Palley
Charles & Donna Scott
Justin Shinebourne
Richard & Julie Slater
The Tracy Family
Leo & Susan van der Linden
Rob Wallace

Great Friends
Tim & Caroline Clark
Robyn Durie
Maureen Elton
Jenny Hall
Susan Hyland
Tony Mackintosh
Ian McKellen
Frank & Helen Neale
Georgia Oetker
Anthony & Sally Salz
Mr & Mrs Bruce R. Snider
Donna & Richard Vinter
Jimmy & Carol Walker

INGENIΘUS is proud to continue its creative partnership with the Young Vic supporting another season of exciting theatre.

Giving a voice to young talent

Land Securities is proud to sponsor the Young Vic

I Am Yusuf and This Is My Brother

Characters

Yusuf, *who has a good heart*

Ali, *his brother, a young man – yellow*

Nada, *a young woman, big black eyes and calm as the sea*

Nagi, *wears glasses and carries a book everywhere*

Rufus, *has two sticks, one in his hand, the other up his rear . . .
and homesick*

Old Yusuf, *like Yusuf but old, around seventy-five*

Abu Salhe, *a rebel leader, tough as nails*

Old Nada, *like Nada but around seventy-five; the sea has dried
but the seashells are still there*

Man with Tree, *a man carrying a tree or a tree holding a man,
hard to tell which*

Old Hag, *as close as possible to a goat*

Man from Haifa, *frightened but hiding it*

Woman from Haifa, *has lost everything and it shows*

Dead Refugees, *who all move as fast as geckos*

Prologue

2000

A house in Ramallah.

Sitting around the table are **Old Nada** *and* **Old Yusuf.**

Ali *is there all through the scene sipping his tea silently.*

Old Nada   Bath!

Old Yusuf   No.

Old Nada   You must!

Old Yusuf   I hate water.

Old Nada   Yusuf, you have to.

Old Yusuf   No.

Old Nada   Yusuf, we've talked about this.

Old Yusuf   The water is cold. Ali, explain to her.

Old Nada   I told you not to do that!

Old Yusuf   Ali, Ali, Ali, Ali, Ali . . .

Old Nada   Listen to me. Don't do that!

Old Yusuf   You see? She's always telling me what I can do. I'm not allowed to talk to my own brother.

Old Nada   Stop it at once. You know better then that! What has Ali to do with you needing a bath? You smell. Leave him in peace and get ready.

Old Yusuf   I want more tea.

Old Nada   It's your fifth cup! Stop bargaining for time!

Old Yusuf   Time? We give no time, we take no time. (*He giggles.*) Last night they never stopped shooting. The army came all the way into the centre. The boys stoned them, right here in Manara. I can't go into the street, right? So why take a bath?

Old Nada   *Because* you can't go out. *Because* we're stuck in the house and I will not allow you to smell! The curfew's bad enough.

Old Yusuf   Fine, so Ali should have a bath as well.

Old Nada   Enough! Get up and go take a bath.

Old Yusuf   Ali, help! She's hurting me!

Old Nada   Sorry, I didn't mean . . .

Old Yusuf   She wants to drown me.

Old Nada   What did you say . . . ?

Old Yusuf   You heard . . . Ali, help me!

Old Nada   God forgive you! I've spent my life taking care of you. And . . . after Ali . . . You should be ashamed.

Old Yusuf   Ali, Ali, Ali . . . Give me your hand! I'm falling! Your hand!

Old Nada   Shhh. Breathe in, breathe out. Shhh. We don't need a bath. It's OK. No bath today . . .

Old Yusuf   I can't breathe! The water's in my nose, in my lungs! Ali! Air, I need air! The water's black, it's cold. I'm all alone. I hear the echo. Yusuf − suf − suf − suf − suf −

Old Nada   Here . . . Breathe in, breathe out. Hold me.

Old Yusuf   I hate water! I'm drowning! She's drowning me!

Old Yusuf *bites* **Old Nada**, *drawing blood.*

Old Nada   Ahhh . . . Curse you! Let go!

Ali   Let go, Yusuf.

Old Nada   Let go, Yusuf!

Old Yusuf   Suf − suf − suf . . . I'm falling . . . Nada, help me. Nada!

Old Nada   Shhh . . . I'm not leaving you, I'll be back.

She goes out.

Old Yusuf   Ali, you left me. I'm in the well. I found her, you left me. It's cold in here. It's dark.

Ali *pins* **Old Yusuf** *to the ground.*

Old Yusuf   But I see your head and the blue sky. Your head, Ali, surrounded by pigeons, a whole flock, grey and white. I hear my name. If you'd listened to me, Ali, even just once. I told you she'd be here!

Old Nada *comes back, pressing a hanky to her hand. She sees* **Ali** *and stands amazed.*

Act One

The village of Baissamoon. A day full of dust and sun.

Young Yusuf *runs away from* **Ali**, *who catches him and flings him to the ground.*

Yusuf Be sorry for me.

Ali No!

Yusuf Don't be angry with me.

Ali Why were you born? Good for nothing! Why? I should have drowned you like a puppy.

Yusuf Oh, I like puppies.

Ali *hits him.*

Yusuf Ahhh!

Ali The whole village laughs at me.

'There goes Ali and his stupid brother.'

Yusuf I did nothing! I counted the coins in my pocket, that's all.

Ali *slaps him.*

Ali They see me, they laugh.

Yusuf I didn't say anything. Ahhh!

Ali I want to do so many things. I have such big dreams.

Yusuf You only have one dream – Nada.

Ali You, shut up.

Yusuf Ahhh!

Ali If it wasn't for you, I'd have her. But it's a disgrace to have us in their family. Her father said that to my face: 'You marry my daughter? How do I know your children – my grandchildren! – won't be like Yusuf?'

Yusuf If they are, I'll have someone to play with! I'll teach them to pick figs . . .

Ali If they are, I'll drown them like puppies.

Ali *gives* **Yusuf** *a blow that sends him to the ground. He kicks him, then sits on him, still hitting him.* **Yusuf** *speaks during this.*

Yusuf When my brother hit me, he always had a reason.

I tried to focus my ideas . . . ignore the pain . . .

If my coins fell out of my pockets

I'd watch them roll and glitter in the sun . . .

The metal ringing on the rocks . . .

They race each other like galloping horses . . .

Pick up speed . . . do a silly dance . . . wobble . . .

Then lie still . . .

Like me . . . breathing in and out . . .

That made me feel better.

When my brother hit me, he always had a reason.

He was sorry for us, that's what it was . . .

Ali *collapses near* **Yusuf**, *sobbing.*

Ali He was laughing at me, her pig of a father. And Nada just sat there, her eyes making love to the carpet.

Yusuf They have nice carpets . . . Stop it, don't hit me, be sorry for me, I'll change!

Ali Change? You can't, you can't . . .

RUFUS

Enter **Rufus**, *a solder in the British army.*

Rufus   Oh, my good lord. What on earth are you doing to this man?

Ali   Me? Nothing, what am I doing? *What does he want now?*

Yusuf   *I don't know. To give us chocolate?*

Rufus   You can't behave like this. Get off him.

Ali   *You want us to get something sweet for you and something to smoke for me? So scream loud . . .*

He punches **Yusuf.**

Yusuf   Ahhhhhhhhh!

Rufus   Stop that now! Do it!

Ali   He my brother!

Yusuf   He brother my. Me name Yusuf. He Ali.

Ali   *Shut up. You'll cock it up.*

Rufus   You're brothers? Typical. (That's the whole problem.) Stop hitting him. Get off, for God's sake! Do it!

Ali   He family of mine. In my family I do what I want, yes? Or is King of London want to come between brother of me and me?

Rufus   King of England! Idiot. It's too bloody hot for this. Get off him!

Ali   No.

Yusuf   No. *Look, he is becoming red like a tomato.*

Rufus   What did he say? Come on, mate, get off him – I'll give you some chocolate. There's enough for both of you.

Ali   Cigarette. Me want cigarette.

Rufus   OK, a cigarette for you and chocolate for him. Just get off!

Ali   Yes, cigarette good. But I need to sit on him. I still
mafashets guli. He dangerous, crazy, he bite you and eat all
chocolate and then we in trouble with King of London!

Rufus   King of England! Say 'King of London' one more
time and I'll sling your arse into the jail at Acre with the rest
of you bloody . . .

Ali   You no good get angry! Get hot, get red!

Yusuf   Chocolate! Mr Chocolate!

Ali   He so strong, I hold, give chocolate, go. He bite, very
strong . . .

Rufus   OK, OK. It's the King off . . .

Ali   Lon . . . gland

Rufus *exits.* **Ali** *climbs off* **Yusuf***. Now they are like two cubs
playing.*

Ali   Eat.

Yusuf   Tasty.

Ali   Finish. We have to go on.

Yusuf   Doing what?

Ali   Hitting you.

Yusuf   Wait. I don't get chocolate every day! God save the
King of London

Yusuf   God save the King of London.

Ali *smokes his cigarette, puffing at* **Yusuf** *who pretends to choke.*
Yusuf *offers* **Ali** *chocolate but never lets him take any – it's a game.*

Ali   That's it! Time's up!

Ali *climbs back on him, both laughing.*

Yusuf   'Going fast is the devil's speed!'

Ali   Oh, don't start that again.

Yusuf   Your turn.

Ali   That's the one thing we're good at – proverbs. 'What you eat, that's what you are.'

Yusuf   Good one! 'Smoking starts cool then you find you're the fool.'

Ali   All right. 'You can run till you drop but you're still for the chop.'

WOMEN

A line of **Women** *walk to the well, singing. All carry jars on their heads.*

Women
Like stone our water is cold
Like shadow it is dark
My waters are captive in a jar.
A stranger stands in a field
And my water and my lips
Long to feel his mouth.

The line of **Women** *walk out.* **Ali** *and* **Nada** *enter.*

Ali   We'll leave. We'll go to Haifa. It's a big city. No one will find us.

I'll work in the port day and night. I'll work like a dog . . .

You and me and Yusuf . . . We'll have a small house . . . We don't need a lot. Since we were small, and nobody else and more then anything.

Yusuf   Nada . . . I'll stand guard. Talk! Talk!

Nada   Leave everything behind?

Ali   Yes, leave. At night we'll walk on the beach! The sea, did you ever see the sea?

Nada   Once but I didn't swim. I wasn't allowed to.

Ali   This time you will be allowed to.

Yusuf Everything's OK. No one's coming . . .

Ali And we can have a soda. You know what soda is?

Nada No.

Ali It's sweet water with bubbles in it. Sweet like you.

Nada With bubbles like you.

Long pause.

Ali Nada . . . Let's run. Haifa is so big; there are cars and a train. Have you ever seen a train? We – me and you and Yusuf . . .

Nada How can we leave? Just go? My brothers, my family, my mother?

Ali Just go! Haifa has gardens and streets and cafés. People come from all over the world to be there. Haifa is so big they'll never find us. We'll make it. I'll work. And you and Yusuf can take care of the house. He'll help you with everything.

He loves you . . .

Old Yusuf He loves you . . .

He hugs her.

Ali Get lost.

Nada Ali, my hands are tied.

Ali We can run! We can cut the ties!

Nada You're crazy.

Ali And seeing you marry someone else isn't crazy? What do you think will happen if we stay here? They will marry you off to someone else.

Nada I'll slit my wrists before that happens. Ali, nothing's changed.

Ali Your father's changed, the whole village's changed, we've changed!

Nada   Time's on our side. I'll say no to everyone. He'll have no choice.

Ali   Me and Yusuf, we'll leave . . . No reason to stay here. Tell me now, are you coming with us?

Nada   Ali, why? Since we were small and nobody else and more than anything –

I can't! I can't!

Ali   We'll leave.

Nada   Then leave . . . but remember I'll always be here waiting.

Ali   Nada –

Nada   What?

Ali   Don't wait.

Nada   When I see you I feel like someone's hit my head with a stone, like someone's put his hands inside me and is ripping out my lungs. When I see you, I . . .

Since we were small, and nobody else, and more than anything.

She runs out.

Yusuf   She loves you.

Ali   Did she tell you anything?

Yusuf   She didn't. But I know.

Ali   What do you know?

Yusuf   About love, I know about love. It's like . . . it's when . . . I love you, right? So it's the same but a boy and a girl, they do other things . . .

Ali   It's all your fault.

He runs out.

Yusuf   It's my fault . . .

I must change. I want to change . . .

It's my fault, it is . . .

Old Yusuf   Shh, breathe. It was never your fault . . . never.

> *'Allah rewards the charitable. He said: "Do you*
> *know how you treated Yusuf and his brother*
> *when you were ignorant?" They said: "Are you*
> *indeed Yusuf? He said: "I am Yusuf and this is*
> *my brother."'*

Nagi *comes in.*

Nagi   That was good. Go on, go on.

Yusuf   Nagi, teach me.

Nagi   Not now

Yusuf   I have a question.

Nagi   What do you want to know?

Yusuf   Why can't I be like the others?

Nagi   It's not possible to have everything like you want it. Some things can't be different from how they are.

Yusuf   But Ali . . .

Nagi   Ali and Nada is one of them. No one can change that. And you can't change yourself. Even if you became like everyone else in the village, you're the village fool – that's who you are, like I'm the newspaper man.

Yusuf   Even if you stop telling people the news?

Nagi   Even when there's no news left to tell. Who hears what I say? They like to hear my voice and see a white piece of paper, that's all. You're different. You're hungry for news. You long to know what's going on. True? Sit. So, today's lesson. The political situation in Palestine after the collapse of the Ottoman Empire . . .

Yusuf   No, not politics! Tell me proverbs. That's what I like!

The following overlaps – **Nagi** *keeps on talking while we hear* **Yusuf.**

Nagi   Yusuf, people say the proverbs because inside them is truth. People talk politics because it's a lot of lies. They're the same – only opposite. Now, focus your ideas. The political situation in Palestine after the collapse of the Ottoman Empire was a shambles. The League of Nations gave the British . . .

Yusuf   Nagi taught me how to write my name in the sand. And he taught me how to recite the Koran! He taught me every one of the proverbs I know. He taught me everything.

Nagi   Then the Crusaders . . .

Yusuf   My father laughed at him, said if he likes wasting his time, after me he can start teaching the chickens. So just to prove to him I'm *not* a waste of time, Nagi bet my father he can teach the rooster to dance *debbka* in a week!

Nagi   Then the Turks . . .

Yusuf   They shook hands. Father said if by next Thursday the rooster can dance *debbka* – or waltz or tango – he will give him our male goat. By next Thursday!

Nagi   The Brits . . .

Yusuf   My father laughed and said Nagi went to university an ass and came back a mule.

What is university? Why do people do it to themselves? I don't know.

On Thursday the whole village came, everyone was there.

Nagi   And now – these . . .

Yusuf   Nagi took two crates, put a sheet of metal between and draped a sheet across.

My father stood up and said: 'Nagi, if the rooster doesn't dance, I'll let you off. Solomon the wise had the gift of speaking with animals but you have the patience of a piece of wood under the saw.'

Everyone clapped. Then Nagi said: 'Abu Ali, if the rooster dances, you can keep the goat. What I want is that you let me teach Yusuf.'

My father hugged me smiling and said: 'Instead of a goat you'll get a lamb.'

They were all looking at me. I was so proud.

Nagi said *bissmillah* and asked everyone to sing *ya hallahe* but very slowly because even *this* rooster is only a rooster. Then he said: 'The rooster is shy so I'll hide under the table.'

Everyone started to sing. And then – *Allah hu Akbar* – the rooster began to dance! Very slowly. It lifted one leg, then the other, then the first . . . All eyes on the rooster – and only me, the fool, crawled under the table to look for Nagi and tell him it had worked.

Nagi sat under the table holding a candle in each hand, heating the metal under the feet of the rooster . . .

Nagi   Yusuf! You're daydreaming! Put that bread in your pocket. It's not time to eat!

Yusuf   I'm hungry!

Nagi   Did you hear anything I told you?

Yusuf   You were talking about . . . ahhh . . . the . . . UN that is going to . . . going to . . .

Nagi   Vote on the partition plan! Focus your ideas!

Yusuf   Partition?

Nagi   Our land! They're going to cut it into two parts. One for us, one for them. But everyone knows: give them one part, they take it all. Everyone knows, if the plan goes through it means one thing – war.

Yusuf   How can you cut up a country?

Nagi   They can. They draw a line in a map and what was one becomes two

Yusuf   Like a loaf of bread?

Nagi   A loaf of bread with sour cheese.

Yusuf   But that's stupid. If you take half my bread I'll be hungry.

Nagi   We'll all be hungry.

Yusuf   No, you can have my half.

He gives it to him.

Ali *comes in, very angry.*

Ali   Nagi, what can I do? He's going to ruin her life and mine. And why? Fear of what people will say. He's a coward.

Nagi   Calm down.

Yusuf   Nada's father? A coward? They say in '36 he stopped the English from arresting all the men in the village.

Ali   '36, '36. How many times must I hear about '36?

Nagi   Calm down. (*To* **Ali**.) Not now, Yusuf

Yusuf   People say that . . .

Ali   People say you have a devil inside you.

Yusuf   Do I?

Nagi   You don't. Ali, don't dare . . .

Ali   You talk to him. You're educated, he'll respect you.

Nagi   Fine. But, listen to me. If we stay calm, everything can be resolved. I'll go. But let's see if he's as bad as you say. You sit down and don't you dare hit your brother. (*To* **Yusuf**.) Calm him down.

He exits.

Ali   'Your brother is a problem . . . Your brother is the problem.'

Yusuf   I will go. I will change.

Ali   It's not about you. You're different and here everyone wants to be the same. Look at their moustaches, all the same. In '36, in 1900 . . . All they want is their stupid stories of how generous they are, how brave they were . . . Whatever happens, we can't go on like this. I'll go and talk to him.

Yusuf   Don't go . . . If Nada –

Ali   I have to! Nagi can't do this job for me.

'Every man must pluck his own thorns.'

Yusuf   'Jars can break jars.'

Ali   What?

Yusuf   'You tried to put on make-up and poked out your eye.'

Ali   Yusuf, I love you . . . I have to go.

Yusuf   No!

Ali   You won't change my mind.

Yusuf   Listen, . . . 'What do you want? To steal grapes or to fight the man who guards the vineyard?'

Ali   Both! I want both!

Ali *exits.*

Yusuf   I can teach her . . . Tell Nada to act crazy like me just for a week then he'll give her to you. I can teach her . . . 'Grapes are sour, grapes are ripe.' Why does no one listen to me?

RADIO

Rufus *comes in, holding a radio.*

Rufus   Hello!

What's the matter? You seem upset!

Your ignorant brother been hitting you again?

Don't want to talk? That's OK. Only reason I'm here is it's a good place to listen to the broadcast, high up, good reception. Every time I want to hear some music in this sodding place I have to drag my radio up here. Lovely thing, a radio. You always feel close to home. I love music, all kinds . . . classical,

swing – but especially opera. I picked that up when I was
stationed in Italy.

Lovely place, gorgeous women.

So let's see what we can find. Do you like music?

You don't follow a damn word I say, do you?

Never bothered me before. Don't know why it gets to me
today.

Wait . . . Here, you try . . .

He presses various buttons on the radio.

If I stand like this, it might just . . .

Oh, *Norma*. I love this: '*Casta diva . . .* '

Shit, it's gone! Shit.

Amazing thing, tonight the whole country's listening, the
whole bleeding world.

The UN voting on the partition plan. If they say yes, we're
going home – hurrah! – and you lot are . . . screwed.

I'm from Sheffield. Nice place, weather not great but, you
know . . .

Everyone loves their own home, don't they?

If I could find the stupid station . . .

Do you mind? Here, like this – lift your hand . . .

Oh great, we've found it.

Music is heard: 'Casta diva' from Norma. **Rufus** *tries not to move,
holding up the radio antenna.* **Yusuf** *starts smiling and gently moving
around.*

The others come in.

Om Samar   Why does she shout like that? What are they
doing to her?

Ali   Tell him we want to hear the news!

Rufus *and* **Yusuf** *see everyone watching.* **Rufus** *is embarrassed.*

Rufus   We were looking for the station . . . the UN voting on the partition plan . . .

Well done, lad, thank you for helping . . . Move along . . .

Nagi   Mr Rufus, can we hear the broadcast?

Rufus   Yes, of course. Yusuf, give me a hand

Om Omran   It won't pass. You can't divide a piece of land!

Ali   If it does the blood will pour.

Nada   But if they pass it?

Ali   It will pass.

Om Omran   It won't pass because we don't agree.

Nagi   It won't pass – America is on our side !

Rufus   Shhh . . . shhh . . . the voting, the broadcast . . .

A recording of the actual vote is heard.

Afghanistan	No
Argentina	Abstained
Australia	Yes
Belgium	Yes
Bolivia	Yes
Brazil	Yes
Belarus	Yes
Canada	Yes
Chile	Abstained
Soviet Union	Yes
United Kingdom	Abstained
United States	Yes

Uruguay	Yes
Venezuela	Yes
Yugoslavia	Abstained
Yemen	No

The resolution of the Duke Committee for Palestine has been adopted by 33 votes for, 13 against and 10 abstentions.

Long pause. Everyone looks shocked as they walk out. **Nagi** *gives* **Yusuf** *a piece of bread.*

Yusuf   Did it pass?

Nagi   It passed

Yusuf   You said it won't.

Nagi   But it did.

Yusuf   What is it?

Nagi   The bread you gave me. I'm not hungry any more.

Ali *and* **Nagi** *exit. During the speech that follows,* **Old Yusuf** *comes in, stands at the back and picks up the lines.* **Rufus** *and one of the village girls are in the back, listening to a romantic song and flirting.*

JANUARY

Old Yusuf   They drove up in jeeps. Men and women also. They parked behind the low hill where Salma showed me her knees one day when we were alone. They had guns with long barrels.

Yusuf   They walked around talking quietly.

Her knees were white. She also showed me her thigh. I felt funny.

Old Yusuf   Salma said: 'Don't tell a soul . . . '

One of the men was very blond.

Yusuf He sweated a lot –

Old Yusuf – and kept patting his forehead pointing here, there . . .

Yusuf I stood silent on a branch trying not to breathe.

Old Yusuf A thin man with big sad eyes looked at the tree I was hiding in. Our frightened eyes met. I said: '*Ashad ana la illaha*', but he turned his head, pointed somewhere else.

Yusuf I didn't finish the '*el allah and muhamed rasul allah*'. I couldn't do it with my fingers because my hands were gripping the branch.

Old Yusuf They pointed their guns at the ground and did something that made a noise like a key in a door . . . They got into their jeeps. Salma was fat . . .

Yusuf – very fat. They drove away in a cloud of white dust –

Old Yusuf – white like Salma's thighs.

Yusuf Now she's married to Ajami, the mechanic at the refinery in Haifa –

Old Yusuf – she's even fatter . . . We saw them first in January, then all the time. They invaded our dreams, our conversation –

Yusuf – the salt on our bread –

Old Yusuf – the water in our jars. Now everywhere I see those big sad eyes.

Yusuf Before January, who knew they existed?

Old Yusuf After January, who is sure that we do?

Her thighs were so white . . .

Yusuf White . . . so white.

Act Two

Nagi Is this a good revolver?

Abu Salhe It will do the job.

The best time is to get him in Amuka.

Nagi I know him. We are neighbours.

Abu Salhe The moment the meeting is over you do it. One clean shot.

Nagi But if they come after me?

Abu Salhe They won't. They won't risk themselves for him. He's a dog.

Nagi You sure this revolver is good? It's very rusty.

Abu Salhe I told you, it will do the job.

There is somebody coming. Nagi, we trust you.

Abu Salhe *runs out.* **Rufus** *walks in.*

Rufus Mr Nagi . . . Everything OK?

Nagi Yes. Why?

Rufus Just checking. It's my job. We've had reports that the Qaougji rebels are kicking up trouble.

Nagi We call them the Qaougji warriors.

Rufus What's the exact point you're making?

Nagi Well, there're none in our village. We're a tiny village at the end of the world. Nothing happens here.

Rufus I hope it stays like that. In some areas things are heating up.

Nagi And that's nothing to do with you?

Rufus What do you mean?

Nagi You are allowing many bad things to happen.

Rufus Not true. We don't take sides. But if anyone's responsible, it's you. If you'd agreed to the partition, none of this would have happened.

Nagi Mister, can you give me your left hand? Can you give me your right leg?

Rufus I don't understand.

Nagi They belong to you, but can I have them – to keep?

Rufus No.

Nagi Have a good day.

HAIFA

A **Man** *and a* **Woman** *come in.* **Ali** *and* **Yusuf** *help them with the bundles they carry. The* **Woman** *walks as if asleep.*

Ali Here you are. Rest in the shade. Let me take this.

Yusuf What is it? What's in here?

Ali Yusuf!

Man It's OK. It's everything we had.

Pause.

Ali Yusuf, bring something to drink, and food.

Man Water, just water . . .

Yusuf Water!

He exits. **Ali** *stares at them. Long pause.*

Woman Haifa. We're from Haifa.

Ali I didn't ask.

Woman Your eyes did.

Ali   Sorry . . .

Pause.

Woman   Tell him . . .

Man   If he asks.

Woman   He needs to know

Man   If he asks

Ali   I'm asking.

Man   We left because . . . You see . . . What's the good of staying, you see? Our house was on the edge of no man's land, where all the fighting is taking place and my daughter . . . she didn't want to stay. I wanted to stay and fight but she, you see, isn't feeling so good . . .

Woman   Tell him about the snipers . . . About the dogs . . .

Man   Snipers, the worst is the snipers. You want to get from here to there, they wait till you've gone half way then they shoot.

Woman   About the dogs . . .

Man   The dogs. There are lots of dogs running wild . . . Dogs driven mad by the never-ending shooting. Dogs of every breed. They hang around the no man's land, you know, eating . . .

Woman   Tell him . . .

Yusuf *comes in with water.*

Ali   I'd rather he doesn't.

Man   Yes.

Ali   Bring something to eat, anything.

Yusuf   But, but, but . . .

Ali   Fly like the wind.

Yusuf *goes off.*

Woman   Tell him everything about the dogs.

Man   The dogs rule the streets. The English have withdrawn to the port. The city's ready to collapse, that's the truth . . . Any day now. Or maybe a week or a month but we've lost . . . Our warriors leave by night. Silently, but we know they're leaving . . .

Woman   Why won't you tell him?

Man   She's not feeling so good. I'm sorry . . .

Woman   Tell him . . . what the dog did to Amer! Your son, my brother.

Man   We don't know what happened!

Woman   We saw a dog, a German shepherd, Amer's shirt in his mouth . . . The kids go to no man's land, they get excited, their little hearts beat strong . . . When they're shot a lot of blood gushes out.

Man   Please stop.

Woman   It gushes out, calling the dogs. They hear the cry of blood. They always come. That's what I want you to tell him about the dogs.

Man   We don't know, maybe he's lost, maybe he's at his uncle's house in Rusmihha?

I'm taking her north, then I'll go back . . . He's in his uncle's house in Rusmihha. He's only ten. He's waiting for me . . . He must be frightened . . . Come, we have to hurry.

Carry this . . . Thank you.

Woman   Go before they get you. Go . . .

*The **Man** and the **Woman** leave.*

Ali *sees them off, then retches, gasping for air.*

Yusuf *comes in running, holding a pinch of salt.*

Ali *pulls himself together.*

Yusuf   Where did they go? Here's the salt!

Ali   They had to go.

Yusuf   Why?

Ali   They had to go.

Yusuf   Where were they from?

Ali   Haifa.

Yusuf   The sea! Will you take me to the sea? Promise!

Ali   Soon. It's a wonderful city – the dove of the sea. Full of gardens and cars. We'll drink coffee . . . ride a bus. The dogs . . .

Yusuf   What?

Ali   People in Haifa walk the street with their dogs on a leash. And we can . . . The dogs . . . we can . . . the dogs . . .

Yusuf   Pat the dogs?

Ali   Yes, I couldn't find the word.

He is about to vomit. **Nagi** *comes storming in.*

Yusuf   Nagi, there were people from Haifa . . . and Ali couldn't say 'pat'. I could.

Nagi   Go on, go on. (*To* **Ali**.) We have to talk! What did you do? You are so stupid.

Ali   What?

Nagi   So you went to his house and called him a coward. It's lucky you got a slap and not your throat cut.

Yusuf   He slapped you?

Nagi   I can't help you any longer. Watch whose toes you step on . . . Nada's father can be dangerous.

Ali   I don't care!

Nagi   Oh? But will you care when I tell you he dragged Nada by the hair through the village. All she did was mention your name.

Pause.

Ali   I'm going to kill him! Feed his belly to the dogs!

Nagi   Where are you going? ! Don't be crazy!

Yusuf   Ali, stop. Please stop, I beg you.

Ali   Get off me. The dogs, I'll feed him to the dogs!

Ali *gives* **Yusuf** *a blow that sends him to the floor.* **Nagi** *runs after him.* **Yusuf** *struggles to recover.*

Yusuf   Everyone thinks 'poor old Ali' because he's my brother. No one thinks 'poor old Yusuf' . . .

No one thinks 'poor old walls' that have to hold the roof on their back, grinding their teeth. The walls are hurting.

No one thinks 'poor old jars', they're cold from the spring water. But they're cold and in pain and the water that's trapped inside is in pain, and the salt in my tears is in pain, it's wasted on sorrow, not on bread.

The file of **Women** *with jars on their heads passes. They sing a song.*

Women
   Like stone our water is cold
   Like shadow it is dark
   My waters are captive in a jar.
   A stranger stands in a field
   And my water and my lips
   Long to fell his mouth.

Nada *runs in, in distress.*

Nada   Yusuf, where's Ali?

Yusuf   Oh my God, what happened?

Nada   Where is he?

Yusuf   I don't know . . .

Nada   Tell him I'll wait for him no matter what.

Yusuf   Wait for him –

Nada They're going to send me to my uncle in Amuka.

Yusuf Uncle – Amuka –

Nada So tell him I will wait.

Yusuf You will wait –

Nada He must be careful. My father's looking for him.

Yusuf Careful –

Nada When it's time, I'll let him know. I'll find a way. We'll go, all of us.

My father thinks I went to bring water . . .

I'm ready now. Tell him I will drown –

Yusuf Drown –

Nada He's my man. For him I'll give up everything. He's my water, I'll drown in him. Tell him I will wait.

Yusuf Water –

Nada They think I went to fetch water. I must run. Don't forget.

She starts to go. **Old Nada** *blocks her way.* **Nada** *comes back, looks at him.*

Nada We'll do everything together, everything. I love you too.

She gives him a big hug, runs off.

Yusuf Wait . . . uncle, Amuka, careful, drown, water, you wait –

Wait, uncle, Amuka, careful, drown, water, you wait –

Wait, uncle, Amuka, careful, drown, water, you wait –

Ali, where are you? I don't want to forget. Please God, help me remember.

Wait, uncle, Amuka, careful, drown, water, you wait –

What is that?

Focus, God damn you!

It's so beautiful.

What is it? God damn it!

Ali *comes running in, stands and looks at the sky.*

Ali   Today we saw an airplane!

It flew over the village

From south to east,

Very slowly.

A metal butterfly crossed our sky

For the first time.

Everyone ran out,

Left everything and came,

Salma holding a cup in one hand, a pot in the other,

Khalil carrying a turnip he just picked.

No one knew what to do.

Some people waved,

Everyone excited.

Abu Imran took a rock, threw it at the airplane,

Said 'I hit it, crushed it like a mosquito.'

We saw the rock fall and almost kill Old Anise,

It missed by that much

But she didn't notice,

She's deaf and almost blind.

She looked up,

Shook her head and cried:

'Tffu, Allah curse you, work of the devil.'

We all laughed

Abu Imran said: 'I hit it, crushed it like a mosquito!'

A long time after

People were still looking up,

Imagining they see something,

Pointing in different directions at the sky.

Then there was silence.

People just walked away.

No one said a word but we were all thinking the same thing:

They have airplanes – we have Abu Imran.

We saw an airplane today.

A dragonfly.

Yusuf *and* **Ali** *are alone, looking up.*

Ali   God help us.

Yusuf   That's so beautiful, airplanes are beautiful . . . I love airplanes.

Ali   And the airplanes love you.

Yusuf   Ah, God damn! Nada, she said . . . Ahhh . . .

Wait for uncle in Amuka be careful to drown in water you wait she waits –

Ali   What? What does that mean? Tell me exactly what she said.

Yusuf   Wait for uncle in Amuka be careful to drown in water you wait she waits –

Ali   No, stupid, no. How can you forget? Please tell me!

Yusuf   I didn't forget, I didn't forget! No! No! She spoke really fast.

Wait for uncle in Amuka be careful to drown in water you wait she waits –

Oh God, what was it?

Wait for uncle in Amuka be careful to drown in water you wait she waits –

Ali Calm down. Everything is all right, Calm down, breathe. Here . . . breathe.

Yusuf They're sending her to Amuka to her uncle.

She'll wait for you. That's what she said.

She'll wait and you must wait. She'll let you know when to come. But be careful, her father's looking.

She'll send a sign, then all of us will run away . . .

She said if you're the water she's willing to drown . . .

She waits for you, you wait for her!

NADA'S FATHER IS DEAD

Nagi *comes in, grabs* **Ali** *by his shirt.*

Nagi Good, Yusuf, go on, go on . . . Nada's father, he . . . is dead.

Yusuf What?

Ali It wasn't me. I swear on Yusuf's life. What happened?

Nagi They found him in a field outside Amuka. He's been shot, over and over. They're bringing him here . . . Look, you were with me, do you hear me? They'll come for you! Whatever happens, you were with me.

Ali I did nothing . . . I swear.

Nagi His family will come for you . . . They have to believe you did it.

Ali For what reason?

Nagi   Because people are saying all kind of things.

Ali   Such as?

Nagi   That he sold his land. To them. Before they take it, he sold it. They caught him red handed. So they shot him. He betrayed us – but his family will blame you.

Ali   Shit, shit, shit.

Ali   Nada's father? But he was in jail with all the men in '36,

Nagi   Yes, that's when he sold out!

Yusuf, you say nothing. Don't speak at all. You hear me?

Ali   Shit, shit, shit.

Yusuf   But if someone asks?

Nagi   Forget what you heard.

Yusuf   But I remember. I heard it.

Nagi   Forget it.

Yusuf   No . . . What I remember I remember.

Ali   I must tell Nada it wasn't me. She'll think it's me.

Nagi   You won't tell Nada anything. What will you say – 'I didn't do it but your father was a collaborator'?

Ali   Shit, shit, shit.

Yusuf   I don't remember anything, I forgot what I heard. Everything.

Everyone comes in ominously.

APRIL

Nagi   It's the end of April

And every conversation starts with just two words

Dair Yassin.

A week ago who'd heard of it?

A tiny village somewhere near Jerusalem.

Now it's the only thing we talk of.

Our men mumble 'Dair Yassin' and their sleep is a nightmare.

Our women bake, their fingers push Dair Yassin into our bread.

Children milk the goats, their hands smell of Dair Yassin.

Our nights, our bread, our milk are sour from fear.

Sour from death, sour from Dair Yassin.

And our village has become tiny

And our air not enough to fill our lungs.

It's April but this spring isn't green,

It's bitter as rotting almonds

In what follows, all speak together. It is like a musical piece based on the Shiite mourning ritual.

The soldier took her gold and killed.

It's a mass grave.

You can smell the dead ten miles away.

Houses were pulled down on top of those who lived there.

'Are we next?'

A hundred and twenty people,

It was a massacre,

Every throat is full of mud.

'Are we next?'

Bodies lie rotting in the houses.

A hundred and eighty.

Now every sentence ends in three words: 'Are we next?'

Our village becomes tiny, our air not enough to fill our lungs

Two hundred people

'Are we next?'

Women shot in front of their husbands.

Children shot in front of their mothers.

'Are we next?'

GB PROTECTION

Rufus *comes in.*

Rufus Calm down, all of you!

Will you translate for me? Thank you.

I want to reassure you – please listen – that the authority we were given over this land, over all of Palestine, and which we have held now for many years, means . . . what it means is, that we – and when I say we, I mean the British crown – are, is responsible for your safety, for your welfare and your protection. And we will stand by that undertaking, I assure you. Translate.

Nagi Some lies about the British mandate taking care of us.

Rufus That's it?

Nagi It's a short language.

Rufus The mandate forces have been and will always be one hundred per cent neutral in all their dealings with all the different peoples of this land. We regard the personal safety of each and every one of you as our special responsibility. In all our time in this wonderful country, we've gone to the greatest possible lengths to ensure that you – and everyone else – were fairly treated. Translate.

Nagi Some more lies.

Rufus You're kidding!

Nagi Not kidding!

Rufus We have built bridges, factories, schools, hospitals. We created jobs, opened new roads. In these difficult times we want to re-emphasise our commitment. In the name of the British Government I tell you: you are not alone! The British Empire stands behind you. Five hundred years of achievements stands behind you!

Nagi Yes, behind us. Taking cover!

Rufus What?

Nagi Mr Rufus, we know you. We know even you don't believe these lies! Your people double-crossed us with the Balfour Declaration. You double-crossed us when you opened all our ports to their immigrants. You will double-cross us now, leaving all your weapons in the hands of our enemies. You double-crossed us so often, if I'm not translating this crap it's for your own safety. We may be simple people but we're not completely stupid.

Rufus I could arrest you for this.

Nagi But you won't.

Rufus Because of our friendship, because we want to keep the peace –

Nagi Because in two weeks your mandate is over! The paperwork is too much to do in two weeks. In two weeks you'll sail home to your Sheffield, and not once will you look back to see the mess that you've made, not once will you realise you're can't solve the problems of Europe where it's nothing to do with Europe. We are not a rubbish heap for your guilt, my friend. We're in your Middle East and what you sow here you'll reap in fifty years or a hundred years in your lovely London. We should arrest you but we won't. Because of our friendship, because we want to keep the peace.

Rufus *exits slowly.*

WHAT TO DO!

Om Omarn   Two weeks and the mandate's over. Two weeks!

Nada   War! War will start!

Abu Imran   We have to send the women and children away!

Om Omarn   We must fight!

Ali   Fight with what? Give me a gun and I'll fight! I can't fight with my eyes!

Abu Imran   We should go, all of us, to the borders and wait. The Arab armies will come!

Nagi   No, we must stay! Haifa fell!

Om Omarn   As soon as the English leave, the Arab armies will come.

Nada   May 15th. That's the end of the mandate. Two weeks!

Nagi   Led fell, al Ramlah fell . . . We must stay.

Ali   The Qaougji warriors are in Haifa –

All   Haifa fell.

Abu Imran   I say we stay, keep our heads down and see what happens!

Om Omarn   What about my herds?

Nada   That's madness. We need to leave.

Ali   I'm staying. Better the devil you know.

Om Omarn   A month! That's all. We'll come back in a month!

Nagi   We must stay. Jaffa fell, Haifa fell, Asklan fell.

We're staying here! It's our land. We have to stay.

BLACK

Ali and Nada stand in front of each other for a long time.

Nada   Go.

Ali   It wasn't me.

Nada   Now go.

Ali   Nada . . . I . . .

Nada   I hate you! Who was it then? Who?

Ali   I can't say.

Nada   You don't know?

Ali   I can't say anything.

Nada   Go.

Ali   Nada, I beg you. Something terrible happened to you, terrible, but we're free now. We can start a life, you and me . . . and Yusuf . . .

Nada   I can't. Not with you. Not until you tell me who killed my father. My brothers say you killed him . . . because of me. So *I* killed him. That's what they say. If we run away we make it true . . .

Ali   It's not true. Your father is dead – *allah yerhamo* – but . . .

Nada   I'll wake in the middle of the night, look at you and think: did he? Was it him? Is that what you want? You're sleeping, breathing in and out, I'm thinking: did he kill my father? Your breath will poison my nights; my fear will poison both of us. Is that what you want? Is it?

Ali   No.

Nada   I loved you. I did. But all these bad words, everything that happened, the war – made it all seem wrong . . . Tell me. I will believe you. Who killed my father?

Ali   I don't know.

Nada   So I wake and think: the man I am hugging destroyed my family.

I won't be here tomorrow . . .

Nada *goes out.* **Ali** *is silent then, biting his fist. He vomits one word.*

Ali   Nagi . . .

Exits.

15 MAY

Rufus *is packing a suitcase.*

Rufus   That's it. At last – orders to evacuate. I have to be in Haifa by tomorrow noon. Cold beer, women in stockings, grey skies and pudding. Let them rip each other's throats out. May 15th, I love you. War is geared up, ready to go. They're just waiting for us to bugger off. Since yesterday new orders come flowing in: leave nothing behind – no maps, no documents . . . No memories.

Salma *comes running in, holding the radio.* **Rufus** *looks at her and walks away.*

Rufus   Packed. May 15th – best day of my life.

Salma *starts singing and the line of* **Women** *come in.*

Women
Longing to his lips
My water is cold like stone and dark like shadow
But the water will not wash the blood
The water will not wash the pain.

Shots are heard. The **Women** *drop their jars to the floor.*

Act Three

THE ATTACK ON BAISSAMOON – 25 JUNE 1948

Yusuf *doesn't move. Bullets whistle by. He still doesn't move.*

Old Yusuf *passes through slowly.*

Yusuf   The south army is fighting the north army and the wind blows.

Where is everyone? Hiding in the bushes?

The leaves on the trees are fighting gravity and the wind is fighting the branches

And the urge to howl

Now the Army is attacking from all fronts!

The wheatsheaves fight against their ripeness and the hard working ants.

The stone walls of our houses fight the salt in our tears and the shrubs.

The rain is attacking tears

And the white of our bones bleaches the whiteness of the clouds . . .

Where is everyone? Running through the olive groves?

The tank is attacking the rice on our plates

And the bitter coffee in our tiny rattling cups.

The cows attack the grass and the grass gives shelter to the dead.

The sheep attack our wool coats and the shepherd on the cross

And the donkeys resist forgetfulness with stubbornness.

The machine gun is spreading sesame on my grandmother's bread

And her warm greeting to a passing guest

Where is everyone? Hiding in the wells?

The airplanes are fighting the butterflies

And the silver mosquitoes swarm round the eyes of the dead dog.

The hungry children bite off their elbows to attack their empty stomachs.

The marching army attacks the snakes in the fields with the stomp of their boots

And the hand grenade attacks the hands and the orange fruits on the trees.

Mice attack the flour sacks.

Flowers attack the graves.

Where is everyone? Hiding under their beds?

The bullets race the wasps and my heart is racing its galloping horses

And the pigeons swirl round the white flags that were my mother's dowry sheets

And the blushing blood of her purity is washed by the black blood of dead hens.

Where is everyone? Gone to the dust and the tents over the hills?

Where is everyone? Where are the smells of cooking food?

Where are the greetings and good mornings of this dawn?

Where are the villagers with their sourdough dreams?

Where is everyone? Am I alone? Has time ended?

Is it the beginning? When will it end?

ON THE WAY

Om Samar   Where are we going?

Old Yusuf   Tell them . . . if they leave they will never come back.

Yusuf   If you leave, you won't come back.

Ali   Did anyone see Nada?

Villager   She left on a truck.

Salma   Abu Raffat was killed.

All   *Allah Erhamu.*

Salma   And Majda, the daughter of Yakub el Khori.

All   *Allah Erhamah.*

Om Samar   Where are we walking to?

Yusuf   Take one last look at Baissamoon. It's the last time you see it.

Nagi   We lost. It was that simple.

The Arab armies came – and went.

They marched in, people cheering: 'One week and we're home!'

One week. The armies were on *their* way home, the people strung along the road holding the keys of what once were their houses, wailing . . .

The war was over before it began.

We lost. They won. We lost.

It was that simple.

Yusuf *and* **Ali** *come in. They look tired.*

Yusuf   We should have stayed with the others.

Ali   We're faster without them.

Yusuf   But where are we going?

Ali   North . . . We're going north.

Yusuf   Yes, but *they* went *that* way, we're going –

Ali   It's better for us to be alone. You want to be with them?
Go. They're not far. Me, I'm going . . .

Yusuf   Wait!

They exit.

A line of people pass holding things on their heads.

Old Nada *appears. She is getting ready to hunt.*

Old Nada   A migration began

In the sky, birds flying south to Africa,

On earth, people flying north . . .

Young Nada *runs in.*

Old Nada   Where to?

Nada   What?

Old Nada   Why are you running?

Nada   Let go!

Old Nada   Not yet. Ah, the smell of Baissamoon in your
hair . . .

Nada   How do you know where I'm from? Do I know you?

Old Nada   Not yet, not yet. Ah, the smell of fear! It will
never leave you. He didn't do it. You know that, don't you?

Nada   I know nothing . . . Did he send you?

Old Nada   Who're you asking? Me or you?

Nada   Me. I'm asking me. Let go. I'm too tired to fight you.
Please, let me go.

Old Nada   Don't fight. You're worn out. You're shivering.
Put your head here. Yes, that feels good. Shhh . . .

Nada   I'll sleep but I don't want to sleep. You smell like the
sea.

Old Nada   It's the salt of my sweat mixed with fear howling in the wind.

Nada   I saw the sea – just once. At Acre. I was six.

Old Nada   Yes, I was there with my father. I sat on his lap.

Nada   The boys dived off the walls, brown bodies glistening in the sun.

Old Nada   The scent of the spices, oranges, saffron, anisette . . .

Nada   In my father's lap everything was yellow and blue. I longed to swim like the boys. 'Of course not,' said Father. I should've run from him, leapt off the wall. I should've said 'No' to him! But I sweated on his lap in my blue woollen dress. I've always longed to go back to Acre . . .

Old Nada   To smell the sea, the anisette, feel the palms of your father, dive into the sea . . .

Nada   Are you from Acre?

Old Nada   We all are. It's the gate in and the doorway out. Shh! They're getting closer.

Nada   I have to go.

Old Nada   Yes, you do. There! To the tents . . . In sixty years, look in a mirror. Don't be surprised to see someone you know . . . Now go to the city of tents.

MAN WITH TREE

Yusuf *and* **Ali** *come on.*

Yusuf   I can't walk any more. Are we going back to Baissamoon? Are you crazy? They'll kill us.

Ali   What if she's under the rubble, what if she's begging for me? I have to know. Then we'll go to the city of tents and look there. But what if she's under the rubble?

Be quiet. Hide!

Yusuf Where?

Ali Shhh.

*A **Man** comes in carrying a full-grown tree on his back.*

Man You! Will you help me?

Yusuf Yes, Uncle.

Ali Why?

Man What?

Ali Why the tree?

Man I planted this tree seven years ago. For four years it was too young to bear fruit. A cold winter came, it almost died and took a full year to recover. Then: fruit. My neighbour's children picked it, all of it, long before it was ripe. This tree I've been tending for some time now and only last year did I taste its fruit.

Ali It's a sin to uproot a healthy tree!

Man What happens to me will happen to it. That became clear as I walked out of my house, so I went back and dug it up.

Ali You'll kill it or it'll kill you! Look at the state you're in.

Man I left my house, I left my land, I left my hills, I left my well in the Ibn Amer valley. Where am I going? I've no idea. I'm fifty and I've never once left my valley. Why would I? But now, now I'm going to the plains and the dust. I won't leave my tree. I won't become a small ring in a big trunk.

Yusuf What does that mean?

Man I've rested enough. Help me put it on my back. The enemy is near.

Ali Don't help him. He needs more rest. You won't make it.

Man I'll try.

Ali And then?

Man   I'll replant it. It'll recover and bear fruit. When it's time to go home I'll pull it up it and plant it back where it belongs.

To imagine *them* under its shade, I don't want to . . . Eating chicken, drinking wine! A young couple in love. God, it's beautiful . . . His blond hair and pale skin, her big breast and perfect white smile under my tree, kissing.

And me in a tent in a place I never heard of . . .

His hand on her back, lifting her into the air, laughing . . . They grow old, she'll make jam from my fruit, he comes home from work, lies under my tree, reads the paper . . .

In its shade a birthday party for their eldest son. He'll hang a swing on this branch – it's a good branch, it's a good tree!

Their son is sixteen, he carves his initials in the bark and a heart and a girl's name . . .

That would have made the tree happy, I know.

And slowly my tree forgets me, the smell of my breath, the sound of my tongue . . .

I'm a vague memory, that's all, in the rings at the heart of the trunk . . .

That's too much . . . I won't be a thin ring . . .

Help me. It's a long way . . . if I make it.

You should go too . . . Help me . . .

Ali   Yusuf, you help that side.

Man   Be careful. You hear me? Be careful.

The **Man** *goes.*

Yusuf   Will he make it? It's a big tree

Ali   He will.

Yusuf   What kind of tree is it?

Ali   What do you mean?

Yusuf What kind of fruit?

Ali The forbidden one.

Yusuf Did you hear that? Ali, I'm afraid. Let's go.

Ali You go. I'm going back.

Yusuf What?

Ali Climb on that ridge, walk to the next hill, wait. I'll come. Don't be afraid.

Yusuf I won't go anywhere without you.

Ali Go.

Yusuf No.

Ali You'll slow me down.

Yusuf Ali!

Ali Stay here. Sit on this rock.

Yusuf You'll never find her.

Ali Where I lost her I'll find her. Don't move till I'm back. Promise.

Yusuf I promise. I'm frightened.

Ali I'll be back before dawn. If you're frightened, count your coins. Yusuf, my brother, you know what you are?

Yusuf What am I?

Ali A hero.

A man carrying a clock passes very slowly.

YUSUF ON THE ROCK

Yusuf *and* **Old Yusuf** *sitting on a rock.*

Yusuf I'm not afraid! I'm a hero!

Twenty-six and two shillings. Ali . . . Shhh . . . Ali . . .

Please come back . . . I won't move.

Who's that? Is someone there? No?

If there's someone, be careful. Am I mad?

All the bushes are moving.

Old Yusuf It's the birds, Yusuf. It's the time of migration. The branches are heavy with birds flying south. We're fleeing north.

Yusuf Twenty-six and two shillings . . .

I'm a hero . . . I will not move.

My brother will get himself killed . . .

I'm mad, you hear!

Old Yusuf And then what?

Yusuf I'll sit here, the war will end, I'll be behind enemy lines.

Old Yusuf They won't understand you, you won't understand them.

Yusuf I'll sit here till I'm old, till I'm part of this rock.

Old Yusuf Ask the rock if it likes that. Poor rock . . . Yusuf sitting on its head . . . Twenty-six and two shillings . . .

Yusuf Twenty-six and two shillings . . . Ali . . .

Old Yusuf Ali – Ali – Ali – It's an echo. My first brother . . .

Yusuf An echo and pigeons flying round my head, up to the blue sky . . . Just like now . . . But now the sky is dark and I'm *not* falling. I'm sitting on this rock until Ali comes.

Old Yusuf Never make a promise you're going to break.

Yusuf I can't stay here alone.

Old Yusuf You're not. I'm not . . .

Yusuf *runs out.*

Old Yusuf *meets* **Old Nada** – *they pass near each other.*

Ali *enters.* **Old Nada** *wraps her face in a scarf, starts to go.*

Ali Where to, old woman?

Old Woman Running from the Turks!

Run, young man, or they'll capture you and put you in their army.

Ali The Turks? They left forty years ago.

Old Woman So run from the French!

They're outside the walls of Acre.

With his triangle hat, he gallops up on his black horse,

Shouting:

'I'll ride to Josephine . . . through the gates of Damascus.'

But Damascus is burning!

Ali Damascus is burning? Is the enemy there already? Who burned Damascus?

Old Nada The Tartars, young man! Genghis Khan!

Ali You're mad . . . Go north, it's safest.

Old Woman No, no, in the north

The fair haired warriors are galloping fast

In snow-white gowns and red crosses

Rushing to meet Death at Hit-tin

To be plagued by thirst and Saladin.

Ali You mean the Crusaders?

Old Woman Who else?

I watched them wade up through the sea!

They built forts, castles,

Fought, robbed, killed, loved, got bored, and left . . .

Ali I must go.

Old Woman Where?

Ali There . . .

Old Woman No! That's the worst!

Titus Andronicus is there with his legion searching for you!

They're looking for the crucified to nail him up him again!

They left the job unfinished . . .

They'll be happy to practise on your wide shoulders.

You'd be perfect.

Ali Get your hands off me.

Old Woman Give me a kiss.

Ali Leave me alone, crazy hag.

Old Woman Maybe I am mad to stay here all this time.

It was yesterday or a thousand years ago. What's the difference?

Let's hug, just for a moment.

Ali Let go. It's dangerous.

Old Woman Another wave arrives, the new Crusaders! So?

What's it to us, to me?

I saw the helmets of the Mamaluks, the troops of Alexander,

The Assyrian army, Lawrence with his Bedouin brothers,

All of them!

From Solomon the wise to Suleiman the great and some other greats besides . . .

They were here, they left.

Where should I go?

Let me hug you farewell, then *you* go, far.

In a hundred years you'll come back with *your* army,

Lay siege to Acre and say 'Once this was ours . . . '

Ali   Wait, old woman. It's dangerous there. Where are you going?

Old Woman   To be six years old. In Acre. Blue and yellow. To the arms of my father. Where else?

For a moment the **Old Woman** *becomes* **Old Nada** *and then* **Young Nada** *is seen, the two standing together.*

Both Nadas   Run Ali. Save yourself. Run.

They vanish in the mist.

Ali   Wait. . . . wait . . .

Nada! Don't go . . . I need you.

I've been looking for you all day.

I'm seeing things. It's her,

It can't be. Get a grip.

Still, Ali, don't move.

Nada . . . Nada . . .

Answer me. I beg you.

Are you there?

The dogs, here? Surrounding me?

Still, Ali. Don't move.

Ali *is shot.*

And the dogs are coming.

They smell blood . . .

Nada is just behind that hill . . . just behind . . .

TOGETHER AGAIN

Yusuf Ali, can you hear me? It's Yusuf. Don't close your eyes. Oh God, what happened?

Ali I was shot.

Yusuf I couldn't stay on the rock. I was too afraid. Don't be angry . . . Don't close your eyes! Does it hurt?

Ali It's warm. I want to sleep. Let me. No talking. Why're you here?

Yusuf Wake up! You hear me? If you close your eyes, that's it! I'll take you. I know the way. You'll be fine. I'll carry you.

Ali Remember the well? Do you remember the well before we clogged it with earth? The one we had in the back beneath the Safsafa tree?

Yusuf It was dry.

Ali Once it had water. Cold water. Then father clogged it up.

He did it after . . . you fell in.

Nobody knows but . . . it was me . . . it was my fault.

I said you climbed in. You didn't. You almost drowned because of me.

I was too afraid to say so I'm telling you now.

We were playing. I said; 'Look into the well and shout your name.' You were three. You put your head over the edge, shouted: 'Yusuf – Yusuf – '

Yusuf Shh . . . You'll get us killed. Yusuf – suf – suf –

Ali They pulled you out, you were blue. Your head cracked open, full of blood. When you woke you were like this, like you are. I didn't mean to push you. It happened. You were kneeling, your back to me, your head in the well. I don't know why I did it – my hand pushed you. You were our father's favourite. Forgive me . . .

Yusuf   Yusuf – suf – suf – Wake up. Keep talking . . . What
did Father do? Did he belt you? He liked his belt. And his belt
liked us. Wake up! Tell me about Nada . . .

Ali   Just before I was shot I saw her. Will you find her for
me?

Yusuf   I'll find her, but now let's go to the city of tents.

Everyone's gone north.

Wake up, Ali!

> *'So when they had gone off with him and agreed
> that they should put him down at the bottom
> of the pit, we revealed to him: You will most
> certainly inform them of this their affair which
> they do not perceive. And they came to their
> father at nightfall, weeping.'*

The water was very cold.

On the way down I heard a voice shout my name.

Yusuf – suf – suf –

Don't close your eyes!

You did a good thing when you called Father . . .

I shouted, a wet echo called my name and the glitter of the
water . . . shiny knifes, silver snakes . . .

I fell a long time. Looked up, saw blue sky, a flock of white
and grey pigeons circling your head, Ali, flying in circles.

Then into the water, cold, silent . . .

Like now . . .

I forgive you. Wake up! I forgive you.

DEAD REFUGEES

Yusuf *carries* **Ali** *on his back, lost and helpless. A group of dead* **Refugees** *come in.*

Yusuf   You, stop, please . . . Help me . . . He's heavy . . .

He's wounded . . . He was shot. Stop a moment.

Refugee 1   A moment and another moment . . . We can't help, not you, nor him . . .

Yusuf   Ali, tell them . . . Help me! He'll die

Refugee 2   When he does, give him to us. Then go north.

Refugee 3   We'll wait with him until . . .

Yusuf   No.

Ali   My body hurts. There's fire in my belly. Put me down. You're a good brother. They'll wait with me. Go.

Yusuf   Help me. We can all be saved.

Refugee 1   From what? We're already saved from now to the salvation.

Yusuf   You're dead?

Refugee 4   We're heading home. Our war's over. The war is yours. You fight in our name. Die – we don't care.

Refugee 1   At home we stare at the sweaty effort you call life.

Yusuf   You're dead?

Refugee 2   We await the Day of Judgement!

Refugee 4   We await a messiah, a prophet. Someone says: 'It's time, dust your ashes, come forth . . . '

Refugee 2   Till then time won't be measured.

Refugee 3   No more time and its numbers.

1948 since the birth of Christ . . .

1367 since the *hejira* of Mohamed . . .

Refugee 1 356 the sun circles the stars without one single smile.

Yusuf Stop. I'm dizzy.

Refugee 2 No more sun or moon in their orbits.

Just the silence of planets and the grandeur of black space expanding . . .

For that we wait.

Yusuf Please stop.

Ali Let me go. Yusuf, it's over. Please. I'm in pain.

Yusuf Ali, don't go with them. Please, don't.

Refugee 2 Come with us!

Refugee 1 I'm going home to Haifa! I'll prowl till time ends along the roof tiles of my house in Abass Street, above the sea . . .

Refugee 2 I'll go to Tiberius, dissolve in the waves of the Lake of Galilee. Fish will nibble my heels where Christ walks each night across the waves.

Yusuf Go, all of you, leave us alone.

Refugee 4 I'm on the way to Al-Ramlah. I'll hide in the lemon groves, in the icy grass and wait. Salvation . . .

Yusuf Get your hands off him. I'll bite you.

Refugee 2 I'm going to Jerusalem, to the gate of mercy where the beggars wait to see if King Solomon will throw them any change . . .

Yusuf Ali, I beg you, wake up . . .

Ali And I'll be in Baissamoon. I'll become the echo on the walls of Nada's house. The echo in our well.

Yusuf Ali, stop it, wake up!

Take my coins, you can have them!

'I've seen eleven stars and the sun and the moon bow down to me.'

Ali, it's me, Yusuf. I will find her, I will tell her . . .

Ali   I'll wait for her. My eternity falls between two heart beats . . .

Yusuf   Give him more time . . .

Refugee 1   We give no time, we take no time . . . What we do is like trading the wind with the waves . . .

The **Refugees** *gently pick up* **Ali** *and walk away.*

Refugee 1   When your time comes, there on the bank of the wide river, we will kill time together . . . Don't forget, Abass Street, the third house on the left . . . Just above the waves . . .

ME AND MY DEAD BROTHER

Yusuf   Ali ! Ali!

Stretch your legs out as long as your bed . . .

Now it's your turn . . .

Wake up before the dogs get me.

Before I'm back in the well . . . the pigeons, the echoes . . .

Ali, talk to me . . . You didn't go with them . . . You're here.

What about me? What about her?

That's it? You give up?

Come with me, we'll go north to the mountains. They say it snows all year . . .

It's not true there's dust. There's no dust and the tents are big.

She's waiting for you . . . She has nobody, just like we do.

We'll live there for a year then go back to Baissamoon.

A year, is that too long? Compared to eternity?

You two will have children, I'll play with them, we'll clear the well.

It's a sin to clog up a good well.

Ali, it's not funny now . . .

I'm afraid . . .

The echoes are gone. There're no pigeons round your head,

I'm alone.

Ali? I will find her. Don't leave me.

Epilogue

2000

The house in Ramallah.

Sitting round the table are **Old Nada**, **Old Yusuf** *and* **Ali**.

Nada When Yusuf appeared outside the tent, it was pouring with rain. He saw me, he smiled. He was so thin. He'd been beaten. He said it was the enemy but I know it was someone in the camp. I didn't think. I knew what to do.

We've been together sixty years . . .

I missed you . . .

You know, the moment I took him in was the first time I made a decision for myself! I decided you and me *will* be together.

We were so young!

Sixty years, I smelled you in the air.

Sixty years, every shadow was you, was me, was Yusuf.

We carved a life out of mud.

Look at him, sleeping like a child.

He searched for me for two years, in the camps in Syria, in Lebanon. He's stubborn, your brother, as you were.

What's he dreaming about? Look, his lips, breathing in, out . . .

I'm the widow of a man I hardly knew.

I could have married and had a family . . .

For us time stopped that day . . .

'We give no time, we take no time . . . '

They're Yusuf's favourite words. He's got brains, your brother . . .

Old Yusuf Nada, are you here?

Nada   Yes, sweetheart. I'm here. Everything's OK.

Old Yusuf   And Ali? Is Ali there?

Nada   Ali's here . . . And the blue sky and the pigeons are still circling above his head. Go to sleep, sweetheart. Go back to sleep . . .

Black.

Methuen Drama Student Editions

Jean Anouilh *Antigone* • John Arden *Serjeant Musgrave's Dance*
Alan Ayckbourn *Confusions* • Aphra Behn *The Rover* • Edward Bond
Lear • *Saved* • Bertolt Brecht *The Caucasian Chalk Circle* • *Fear and
Misery in the Third Reich* • *The Good Person of Szechwan* • *Life of Galileo* •
Mother Courage and her Children • *The Resistible Rise of Arturo Ui* • *The
Threepenny Opera* • Anton Chekhov *The Cherry Orchard* • *The Seagull* •
Three Sisters • *Uncle Vanya* • Caryl Churchill *Serious Money* • *Top Girls*
• Shelagh Delaney *A Taste of Honey* • Euripides *Elektra* • *Medea*•
Dario Fo *Accidental Death of an Anarchist* • Michael Frayn *Copenhagen*
• John Galsworthy *Strife* • Nikolai Gogol *The Government Inspector* •
Robert Holman *Across Oka* • Henrik Ibsen *A Doll's House* • *Ghosts*•
Hedda Gabler • Charlotte Keatley *My Mother Said I Never Should* •
Bernard Kops *Dreams of Anne Frank* • Federico García Lorca *Blood
Wedding* • *Doña Rosita the Spinster* (bilingual edition) •*The House of
Bernarda Alba* • (bilingual edition) • *Yerma* (bilingual edition) • David
Mamet *Glengarry Glen Ross* • *Oleanna* • Patrick Marber *Closer* • John
Marston *Malcontent* • Martin McDonagh *The Lieutenant of Inishmore* •
Joe Orton *Loot* • Luigi Pirandello *Six Characters in Search of an Author*
• Mark Ravenhill *Shopping and F***ing* • Willy Russell *Blood Brothers*
• *Educating Rita* • Sophocles *Antigone* • *Oedipus the King* • Wole
Soyinka *Death and the King's Horseman* • Shelagh Stephenson *The
Memory of Water* • August Strindberg *Miss Julie* • J. M. Synge *The
Playboy of the Western World* • Theatre Workshop *Oh What a Lovely
War* Timberlake Wertenbaker *Our Country's Good* • Arnold Wesker
The Merchant • Oscar Wilde *The Importance of Being Earnest* •
Tennessee Williams *A Streetcar Named Desire* • *The Glass Menagerie*

Methuen Drama Modern Plays

include work by

Edward Albee
Jean Anouilh
John Arden
Margaretta D'Arcy
Peter Barnes
Sebastian Barry
Brendan Behan
Dermot Bolger
Edward Bond
Bertolt Brecht
Howard Brenton
Anthony Burgess
Simon Burke
Jim Cartwright
Caryl Churchill
Noël Coward
Lucinda Coxon
Sarah Daniels
Nick Darke
Nick Dear
Shelagh Delaney
David Edgar
David Eldridge
Dario Fo
Michael Frayn
John Godber
Paul Godfrey
David Greig
John Guare
Peter Handke
David Harrower
Jonathan Harvey
Iain Heggie
Declan Hughes
Terry Johnson
Sarah Kane
Charlotte Keatley
Barrie Keeffe
Howard Korder

Robert Lepage
Doug Lucie
Martin McDonagh
John McGrath
Terrence McNally
David Mamet
Patrick Marber
Arthur Miller
Mtwa, Ngema & Simon
Tom Murphy
Phyllis Nagy
Peter Nichols
Sean O'Brien
Joseph O'Connor
Joe Orton
Louise Page
Joe Penhall
Luigi Pirandello
Stephen Poliakoff
Franca Rame
Mark Ravenhill
Philip Ridley
Reginald Rose
Willy Russell
Jean-Paul Sartre
Sam Shepard
Wole Soyinka
Simon Stephens
Shelagh Stephenson
Peter Straughan
C. P. Taylor
Theatre de Complicite
Theatre Workshop
Sue Townsend
Judy Upton
Timberlake Wertenbaker
Roy Williams
Snoo Wilson
Victoria Wood

Methuen Drama Contemporary Dramatists

include

John Arden (two volumes)
Arden & D'Arcy
Peter Barnes (three volumes)
Sebastian Barry
Dermot Bolger
Edward Bond (eight volumes)
Howard Brenton
  (two volumes)
Richard Cameron
Jim Cartwright
Caryl Churchill (two volumes)
Sarah Daniels (two volumes)
Nick Darke
David Edgar (three volumes)
David Eldridge
Ben Elton
Dario Fo (two volumes)
Michael Frayn (three volumes)
David Greig
John Godber (four volumes)
Paul Godfrey
John Guare
Lee Hall (two volumes)
Peter Handke
Jonathan Harvey
  (two volumes)
Declan Hughes
Terry Johnson (three volumes)
Sarah Kane
Barrie Keeffe
Bernard-Marie Koltès
  (two volumes)
Franz Xaver Kroetz
David Lan
Bryony Lavery
Deborah Levy
Doug Lucie

David Mamet (four volumes)
Martin McDonagh
Duncan McLean
Anthony Minghella
  (two volumes)
Tom Murphy (six volumes)
Phyllis Nagy
Anthony Neilsen (two volumes)
Philip Osment
Gary Owen
Louise Page
Stewart Parker (two volumes)
Joe Penhall (two volumes)
Stephen Poliakoff
  (three volumes)
David Rabe (two volumes)
Mark Ravenhill (two volumes)
Christina Reid
Philip Ridley
Willy Russell
Eric-Emmanuel Schmitt
Ntozake Shange
Sam Shepard (two volumes)
Wole Soyinka (two volumes)
Simon Stephens (two volumes)
Shelagh Stephenson
David Storey (three volumes)
Sue Townsend
Judy Upton
Michel Vinaver
  (two volumes)
Arnold Wesker (two volumes)
Michael Wilcox
Roy Williams (three volumes)
Snoo Wilson (two volumes)
David Wood (two volumes)
Victoria Wood